# GEORGE WASHINGTON

## Leader of a New Nation

(The Metropolitan Museum of Art, Bequest of Grace Wilkes, 1922)

# George Washington

## LEADER OF A NEW NATION

## Mary Pope Osborne

DIAL BOOKS FOR YOUNG READERS
NEW YORK

Published by Dial Books for Young Readers
A Division of Penguin Books USA Inc.
375 Hudson Street
New York, New York 10014

Text copyright © 1991 by Mary Pope Osborne
Design by Nancy R. Leo
Printed in the United States of America
First Edition
1 3 5 7 9 10 8 6 4 2

Library of Congress Cataloging in Publication Data
Osborne, Mary Pope.
George Washington: leader of a new nation / by Mary Pope Osborne.
p. cm.
Includes bibliographical references.
Summary: A biography of our first President, illustrated with
old prints, maps, and photographs.
ISBN 0-8037-0947-1 (trade). — ISBN 0-8037-0949-8
1. Washington, George, 1732–1799—Juvenile literature.
2. Presidents—United States—Biography—Juvenile literature.
3. Generals—United States—Biography—Juvenile literature.
4. United States. Continental Army—Biography—Juvenile literature.
[1. Washington, George, 1732–1799. 2. Presidents.]
I. Title.
E332.79.O82 1991   973.4'1'092—dc20   [B]   [92]   90-42601   CIP   AC

*For William, Chi Hyon,
and Andrew Boyce*

# TABLE OF CONTENTS

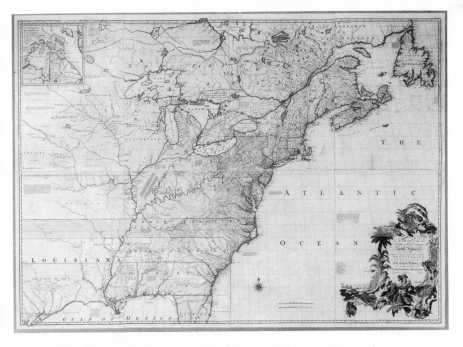

*The thirteen colonies, 1755. (The Library of Congress, Map and Geography Division)*

# INTRODUCTION

AT THE time of George Washington's birth in 1732, France, Spain, and England all claimed land in North America. The land that England claimed was divided into thirteen colonies, and each colony acted as a small, individual country.

But throughout Washington's lifetime many changes came about in North America. England defeated France in the French and Indian War and took over France's frontier lands. Then the thirteen colonies defeated England in the Revolutionary War and became a united country. It was a time for heroes. Historians have marveled at how many great leaders emerged during this period; leaders such as Benjamin Franklin, Thomas Jefferson, James Madison, John Adams, Alexander Hamilton, and of course—George Washington. The time itself seemed to bring forth the highest qualities in these men.

George Washington's greatness lay in his courage and humility. One of his most important gifts to America was his refusal to become a dictator or king after serving as commander in chief of the American army, though many people wanted and expected him to do so. He was a very popular leader and nearly every revolution in history has ended with the popular leader seizing control—leaders such as Napoleon, Lenin, Mao, and Castro.

But Washington did not take advantage of his great popularity by setting himself up as an absolute ruler. This was not part of his vision for a united America. After the war he instead returned to his life as a Virginia farmer. Years later, however, when Washington was *elected* the first president, he felt forced to serve. As James Madison said, "His leadership was the only aspect of the new government that really appealed to people." Finally, after serving two terms, he gladly turned his power over to John Adams.

It's been said that George Washington gained power by giving it up. And by giving up power, he helped America become the free and self-governing nation it is today.

# GEORGE WASHINGTON

## Leader of a New Nation

*Labour to keep alive in your breast
that little Spark of Celestial fire
called Conscience.*

---

From *Rules of Civility and Decent Behavior,*
a childhood book of George Washington's

# Early Years

❦

IN 1675 an Englishman named John Washington left his native country and crossed the ocean to North America. John Washington then settled in America's oldest colony, Virginia. Life was hard and dangerous in Virginia's wild, untamed wilderness. But John Washington, like many other new settlers, built a farm, cleared fields, and planted crops. His son Lawrence did the same. And by the time Lawrence's son, Augustine, was farming, life in Virginia was prosperous and thriving.

Augustine Washington owned a brick farmhouse on the Potomac River in Virginia and on February 22, 1732, a baby boy was born there. The baby was the third son of Augustine and the first son of Mary Ball Washington, Augustine's second wife. Mary and Augustine named their baby George.

Shortly after George Washington was born, Augustine moved his household about forty miles up

Residence of the Washington Family

*George Washington was born and lived in this small house on the
Potomac River in Westmoreland County, Virginia, until he was
three. (The Library of Congress)*

the Potomac River to a larger farmhouse that sat on
a bluff. This farmhouse would someday be called
Mount Vernon. But when George was six years old,
Augustine gave it to his grown son Lawrence and
moved the rest of the Washington household to Ferry
Farm on the Rappahannock River.

At Ferry Farm the Washingtons lived in modest
comfort. Their house had six rooms and thirteen beds.
Travelers going up and down the Rappahannock on

*George's father, Augustine, bought this farmhouse and gave it to his older son Lawrence. It was later called Mount Vernon. (The Library of Congress)*

the ferry often stayed in the extra beds. The Washingtons obtained nearly all their food from their own fields and livestock. They heated their house with fireplaces, and candles lit their rooms at night. Most of their utensils, such as bowls, platters, and ladles, were made of wood, but they prided themselves on having twenty-six silver spoons.

In addition, like most of the Virginia landowners at this time in history, Augustine Washington had black slaves to help run Ferry Farm. At least fifty slaves worked in the fields and in the house.

Not much is known about George's early childhood. An early biographer created the popular fable about him cutting down the cherry tree and then confessing. He probably did play on the banks of the Rappahannock River with his younger sister and three younger brothers. And supposedly one of his favorite games was to pretend he was a soldier like his older half-brother Lawrence.

Fourteen years older than George, Lawrence Washington was a great hero to the young boy. Not only had Lawrence received a good education in England, but he had also distinguished himself as an officer in the Virginia regiment of the British army, fighting in the West Indies.

George expected to follow in his brother's footsteps and be sent to school in England also. But those dreams were shattered when he was eleven years old. At that time his father became ill and died.

After his father's death there was not enough money to send George to England. Because his father's estate had to be divided among seven children, George's share was quite modest. The lack of a good education was to be one of the great sorrows of his life.

After Augustine died, George was hardly able to go beyond elementary school. But the school books that have been preserved show he studied Latin, astronomy, and geometry. He seems to have been especially good at mathematics, which later helped him become a land surveyor.

*George's half-brother Lawrence Washington was fourteen years older than George. (The Mount Vernon Ladies' Association)*

Records show that George also studied the rules of conduct for a gentleman. When he was thirteen, he copied many rules from a book called *Rules of Civility and Decent Behavior*, including:

Wear not your clothes foul, unript, or dusty.

Sleep not when others Speak, Sit not when others Stand, Speak not when you should hold your Peace, Walk not when others Stop.

Talk not with meat in your mouth.

Labour to keep alive in your breast that little Spark of Celestial fire called Conscience.

When George was fourteen, Lawrence Washington arranged a midshipman's post for him on an English navy vessel. But Mary Washington wouldn't allow George to join the navy. George Washington had difficulty getting along with his stern, strong-willed mother and began spending more and more time at Lawrence's home at Mount Vernon. Finally he left his mother's house altogether and moved in with Lawrence's family.

Life at Mount Vernon was quite different from life at Ferry Farm. Lawrence's wife, Anne Fairfax, was a member of the distinguished Fairfax family. The Fairfaxes lived near Mount Vernon on a grand

and elegant plantation called Belvoir. Whenever George visited Belvoir, Colonel Fairfax and his children treated him like a member of the family.

Washington was extremely tall for his age. He had pale skin, reddish hair, and blue eyes. Though he had large hands and feet, and spoke slowly, he carried himself erectly. He was also sensitive and graceful, copying love poems in his notebooks and paying for dancing lessons with his hard-earned money.

One of Washington's most outstanding features was his amazing physical strength. It was said that he could throw a stone across the wide Potomac River or ride six days on horseback without resting. Though these stories may be exaggerated, Washington was an excellent rider. Thomas Jefferson once said that Washington was "the best horseman of his age and the most graceful figure that could be seen on horseback."

At the elegant Fairfax home, George showed off his skill as a horseman by riding with the hounds over the Virginia hills. On one fox hunt he caught the attention of Colonel Fairfax's cousin, Lord Fairfax, who was visiting from England. The powerful, wealthy lord took a great liking to George, and after that they often went fox hunting together.

In colonial days, childhood ended quickly. By the time he was fourteen, Washington was earning some

*Washington and Lord Fairfax often went fox hunting together.*
*(The Library of Congress)*

of his own money by surveying land for Lawrence and his friends. George used his father's surveying instruments—a ruler and a compass—to measure and mark the boundaries of woodlots and crop fields.

The Virginia planters had land fever. Because a man's fortune was based on the amount of land he owned, many had their eye on the uncultivated wilderness to the west. Few people had settled in that area, and traders who returned from it told of wolf-haunted forests, shaggy wild oxen, and fierce Indian warriors.

George was very eager to visit the rugged frontier

country. So when Lord Fairfax asked him to measure some of the vast Fairfax landholdings in the Shenandoah Valley, the sixteen-year-old gladly said yes. Thus began Washington's education in the wilderness.

*At age fourteen Washington was earning money as a land surveyor.*
*(The Library of Congress)*

# A Wilderness Education

ABED FULL of fleas and lice was Washington's initiation into the American wilderness. In a diary he kept on his journey through the Shenandoah Valley, he writes the following about a backwoods lodging:

> We got our supper and was lighted into a room and I not being so good a woodsman as the rest of my company, stripped myself very orderly and went into the bed as they called it, when to my surprise I found it to be nothing but a little straw, matted together without sheets or anything else but only one threadbare blanket with double its weight of vermin, such as lice, fleas, etc. I was glad to get up as soon as the light was carried from us; I put on my clothes and lay as my companions.

*At sixteen Washington went on a land surveying mission to Ohio for Lord Fairfax.*

For most of the rest of the trip Washington slept in the open air. He and his friends caught wild turkeys that they cooked on forked sticks over big fires. They swam their horses over a flooded river and traveled by canoe in heavy rains. One day they were surprised to see about thirty Indians coming from war. The surveyors had a friendly encounter with the Indians, in which the natives danced and played music. George wrote:

> The music is a pot half [full] of water with a deerskin stretched over it as tight as it can and a gourd with shot in it to rattle and a piece of horse's tail tied to it to make it look fine. The one keeps rattling and the other drumming all the while the others are dancing.

Once during the trip the straw that Washington was sleeping on caught fire. Another time a windstorm hit his camp:

> Last night was a blowing and rainy night. Our straw caught fire as we were lying on it, and was luckily preserved by one of our men awaking when it was in such a blaze.

> Last night was a much more blustering night than the former. We had our tent carried quite off with the wind and was obliged to lie the latter part of the night without covering.

Another night "was so intolerably smoky," his diary says, "we were obliged all hands to leave the tent to the mercy of the wind and fire."

Due to his sturdy physique, Washington weathered these hardships successfully. For the rest of his life, in fact, he would survive dangerous and rough conditions. By the time he was twenty-five years old, he had survived malaria, smallpox, typhoid, dysentery, and a serious lung disease. Washington was also astonishingly immune to gunfire. Years later when he fought in the French and Indian War, he was the only officer in one battle not injured—even though two horses were shot beneath him and four bullets went through his coat!

After traveling through the wilderness for thirty-one days in blustery spring weather, George returned home. Since it was necessary for him to find work, he decided to continue his job as a surveyor. For the next three years he was a frontier surveyor throughout the Blue Ridge Mountains. On one trip he wrote to a friend:

*Since you received my letter in October last, I have not sleep'd above three nights of four in a bed, but after walking a good deal all day, I lay down before the fire upon a little hay, straw, fodder, or bearskin . . . with man, wife, and children, like a parcel of dogs and cats; and happy is he who gets the berth nearest the fire.*

With the money he earned from surveying, Washington began buying frontier land. By the time he was twenty, he owned almost two thousand acres in the Shenandoah Valley.

When Washington was nineteen, a great sadness overshadowed his life. His beloved half-brother Lawrence was dying of tuberculosis. At that time people believed that a warm, tropical climate could help cure the terrible disease, so Lawrence decided to travel to Barbados, an island in the West Indies. George interrupted his surveying career to take the journey with Lawrence. It was the only trip George was ever to make away from the continent of North America.

Historians don't know what George suffered emotionally during the trip with Lawrence because he did not write about his feelings in his diary. Rather he wrote about hard winds and squalls, about eating dolphin, and about viewing beautiful fields of cane, corn, and fruit trees. He also wrote that a doctor gave them great hope about Lawrence's condition.

In fact, Lawrence coughed and grew weaker throughout the trip. To make matters worse, George became ill with smallpox. When he recovered, his face was permanently marked with scars. It may actually have been a blessing that George got smallpox then, however. After he survived the disease, he was

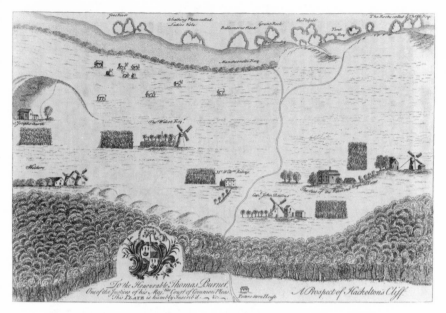

*An engraving of Barbados, 1750. (Beinecke Rare Book and Manuscript Library, Yale University)*

immune to it. Smallpox was later to become the greatest killer of soldiers during the American Revolution.

Lawrence did not survive tuberculosis. In 1752, shortly after his trip to the West Indies with George, he died at home. There's no mention in George's diary of his grief over the loss of his half brother, though he must have been shattered.

In 1754 when Lawrence's widow, Anne Fairfax Washington, remarried and left Mount Vernon, she leased it to George. Seven years later when Anne died, George became the official owner of Mount Vernon.

So at the young age of twenty George Washington found himself the master of a twenty-five hundred acre plantation. He also campaigned to take over Lawrence's post in the Virginia regiment, and—without having had any military training—became a major and began wearing the king's uniform.

Since 1690 the British and French had been competing for lands near the Ohio River. In 1753 Governor Dinwiddie, Virginia's top official, who lived in Williamsburg, received word that the French had built a fort in the Ohio River Valley. The fort was called Fort Le Boeuf.

As the British had already claimed this area, Dinwiddie planned to send a messenger to tell the French that they must leave. It would be a dangerous trip for the messenger across five hundred miles of unbroken wilderness. Winter was also coming soon—rivers would be frozen and canoeing impossible. But nevertheless one man soon volunteered to go on the mission: Major George Washington.

Several men went with Washington on the difficult journey. One of them, Christopher Gist, was an experienced fur trader. Gist not only knew how to navigate the wilderness, but he could also speak different Native American languages.

Another man who was a great help to Washington was Half King, the chief of a Delaware Indian tribe. Half King was eager to help the English fight the

*Governor Dinwiddie of Virginia who, in 1753, sent Washington to Fort Le Boeuf to warn the French to withdraw from British territory. (The Library of Congress)*

French, for he kept insisting that the French had "boiled and eaten his father."

Wearing a buckskin jacket, Washington led his men

and several packhorses through rain and snow into the wilderness. The men had a hard time climbing the ridges of the Allegheny Mountains. As icy and wet winds blew against him, Washington carried a waterproof buckskin pouch inside his jacket. The pouch held a note from Governor Dinwiddie to the French commander at Fort Le Boeuf. The note demanded that the French leave the Ohio Valley at once because they were trespassing on English land.

When he finally arrived at Fort Le Boeuf, Washington changed from his buckskin clothing to his military dress uniform and formally presented Governor Dinwiddie's note to the French commander. After reading it, the commander bluntly declared that the land belonged to the French—not the English. Furthermore, any trespassing Englishmen would be arrested.

Washington was very distressed by the commander's response. He was also upset to see that the French were beginning to form alliances with the Indians in the area. In his diary he wrote, "I can't say that ever in my Life I suffered so much anxiety as I did in this Affair."

Anxious to report back to Dinwiddie at the Governor's mansion in Williamsburg, Washington and Gist decided to leave their party of men and push ahead on their own. During their journey home they were forced to abandon their horses and travel on foot through pathless woods and freezing weather.

*Forced to abandon their horses, Washington and Gist cross an icy river by raft. (The Library of Congress)*

The two men captured an Indian guide who tried to kill them. Then George fell off a raft into an icy river, saving himself only by catching hold of a raft log.

After a month of hard travel Washington arrived in Williamsburg with the bad news: The French were pushing their way into the Ohio Valley.

# The French and Indian War

T HE FOLLOWING YEAR Governor Dinwiddie ordered Lieutenant Colonel George Washington to lead four hundred men in an expedition against the French. Washington and his men hacked a road through the thick wilderness, until they camped in a meadow area. There they built a garrison that they named Fort Necessity.

One day the Delaware Indian chief Half King reported to Washington that footprints of French soldiers had been seen in the woods. Washington gathered a group of soldiers and Indians, and on a rainy night led them in a surprise attack against the camp of Frenchmen. His men easily defeated the French, killing ten of them.

The French were outraged by the attack. They insisted that Washington's men had killed peaceful French diplomats who were on their way to talk to the British. The scandal affected French and English politics even on the other side of the world. Historians have called this small skirmish the first act in a world war. An English politician even described it as "a volley fired by a young Virginian in the backwoods of America that set the world on fire."

*Washington reading prayers in his camp during the French and Indian War. (The Library of Congress)*

Washington, in writing about the skirmish to one of his brothers, had this to say: "I heard the bullets whistle, and believe me, there is something charming in the sound."

Not long after the surprise attack another battle

took place. This time the whistling bullets may not have sounded so charming to the young lieutenant colonel, for the French had convinced a large group of Indians to help them attack the British.

While they fought over the land of the Ohio Valley, the English and French both treated the Indians very unfairly. English and French traders bribed and cheated the Native Americans, stole their lands, and insulted their leaders. But for the sake of their own survival, the Indians wanted to join forces with the side that would win the war. So they finally chose to side with the French. Not only were the Indians angry with the British for building forts on their land, but they were convinced by the French that if the British won, they would become slaves. The French also convinced the Indians that France would soon be sending many soldiers to defeat the British.

On a stormy day in July 1754, when water was flooding the tiny stronghold of Fort Necessity, the French and Indians attacked the British. After a grueling nine-hour battle, nearly one third of Washington's men were dead.

It was still raining at midnight when Washington signed the papers of surrender by the light of a sputtering candle. Soon after this disastrous defeat in the wilderness he resigned his commission with the Virginia militia.

But within six months Washington was back in the war. The king of England had sent General Braddock and his royal troops called "redcoats" to fight the French in the wilderness. When Braddock

*British General E. Braddock led his royal troops, the "redcoats," in fighting the French and the Indians in 1755. (The Library of Congress)*

invited Washington to accompany him as a scout on the march, Washington did not refuse.

General Braddock made sure his men marched to the Ohio Valley in proper British style. He himself rode in a handsome coach over roads cut by his engineers. When the redcoats took the long, rugged trek around gorges and mountain steeps, fife and drum music set a marching beat.

Braddock did not heed Washington's warnings about wilderness warfare. Instead he kept his men marching in the open in rank and file. One July day in 1755, as his soldiers tramped over a twelve-foot-wide trail, the French and Indians ambushed the English army, firing from behind trees and rocks.

Washington tried to persuade Braddock to order the redcoats to charge into the woods after their attackers, but the general refused. A terrible slaughter followed in which the British were so confused they even fired at one another. Braddock was shot through the lungs. After Washington placed his dying commander in a cart, the general is reported to have said, "Had I been governed by your advice, we never should have come to this."

George Washington was the only staff officer not injured that day. He later wrote to his brother that in the battle, "I had four Bullets through my Coat and two Horses shot under me, and yet escaped unhurt."

*Not heeding Washington's advice about wilderness warfare, Braddock
and many of his troops were killed by the French and Indians, 1755.
(The Library of Congress)*

Before dying on the night of the ambush, Braddock ordered Washington to ride forty miles for help. As he moved slowly through the "close shade of thick woods," Washington fell over wounded and dead men.

*The French and Indian troops often ambushed and outmaneuvered the British, who followed traditional battle tactics. Here, Washington witnesses a bloody scene. (The Bettman Archive)*

At times he was forced to crawl on his hands and knees for some of the dark journey. He later wrote, "The shocking scenes which presented themselves in this night march are not to be described. The dead, the dying, the groans . . . and cries along the road of the wounded for help."

When Washington finally reached the second flank of redcoats, the men were too frightened to return with him.

Braddock's defeat was a terrible loss for the British. But it made a hero of George Washington. When he returned to Williamsburg to tell the governor about the ambush, he was honored for his bravery. Soon after, he was appointed commander of all the Virginia troops.

After Braddock's defeat the French and Indian War caused havoc in the Ohio River Valley. Pioneer travel ceased because no one felt safe from Indian fighters in the wilderness. Settlements were abandoned and crops left to die.

For the next two years Lieutenant Colonel George Washington went on different expeditions to the Ohio River Valley, trying to restore order at several frontier forts. In 1759 when the French abandoned their major fort on the Ohio River, Washington retired from the Virginia army and settled at his home at Mount Vernon.

# Gentleman Farmer

*No estate in United America is more pleasantly situated than this. It lies in a high, dry, and healthy country, three hundred miles by water from the sea, and . . . on one of the finest rivers in the world.*

THIS IS HOW George Washington described Mount Vernon to a friend later in his life. But when Washington returned home from the French and Indian War, he needed two things for his plantation. He needed money for house repairs and land expansion. And he needed a loving and agreeable mate to help him run Mount Vernon. In January 1759 he acquired both when he married wealthy Mrs. Martha Custis.

At twenty-seven Martha Custis was the widow of a very prosperous Virginian and the mother of two

*Martha Dandridge Custis at about age twenty-six, in a portrait by John Wollaston. (Washington and Lee University)*

small children—four-year-old Jackie and two-year-old Patsy. Martha was Washington's opposite in many ways. She was barely five feet tall, plump, had small hands and feet, and a very sweet and chatty disposition. Washington, on the other hand, was six feet, two inches tall; large-boned; dignified; and reserved.

After Martha Custis married George Washington, she turned her fortune over to him to manage. This money enabled the Washingtons to enlarge Mount Vernon, to buy more slaves and land, and to grow more tobacco.

For the next sixteen years George Washington was the squire of his plantation. He called everyone who lived at Mount Vernon "his family." This included his wife, his stepchildren, many nephews and nieces, many craftsmen and servants, and hundreds of black slaves.

Historians report that Washington treated his slaves with care. In his will he ordered that all of the Mount Vernon slaves be freed upon Martha's death. Records show that Washington tried not to break up black families. In spite of the consideration he showed his slaves, Washington did not support their immediate freedom. Nor did he grant them more than minimal comforts. Like slaves on all plantations, Mount Vernon's slaves lived in crude log houses and worked hard, long hours, doing lowly tasks.

*The marriage of Martha Dandridge Custis to George Washington took place in 1759. (The Library of Congress)*

Mount Vernon was similar to a medium-sized town. Blacksmiths did all the iron work, making ploughs and other tools. Gardeners planted grapevines and

*Washington and his family at Mount Vernon. (The Library of Congress)*

fruit trees. Shoemakers made shoes. Weavers, spinners, and knitters made clothes and stockings. A miller ran a water mill that ground Mount Vernon wheat into flour. Woodsmen cut timber, and carpenters built new buildings.

Each year the "town" of Mount Vernon produced thousands of pounds of pork, beef, grain, and corn. Tens of thousands of Potomac fish, such as herring and shad, were caught with nets. Cider came from Mount Vernon apple trees. Wine came from its grapevines. Leather and dairy products came from the cows; wool from the sheep; and cotton from the fields.

The goods that the Washingtons couldn't get from their own land, they ordered from England. At that time most Virginia planters sent their tobacco crop to an "agent" in England. The agent sold the planter's tobacco. Then with a portion of the money earned, he bought goods for the planter and shipped them back to Virginia.

Records show that in 1759 Washington ordered two hundred and thirty different household items from his English agents. Among them were: silver shoe and knee buckles for his stepson Jackie; a silk coat and fashionably dressed baby doll for his stepdaughter Patsy; kid gloves and silk hose for Martha; and summer suits and handkerchiefs for himself.

Eventually Washington grew angry with his agents and refused to send them more tobacco. He accused the agents of making poor sales on his tobacco and of forcing him into debt. He also accused them of sending him inferior goods, including clothes that didn't fit.

After a few years Washington decided that growing tobacco not only required too much labor, but it
was not good for his soil. He also wanted complete
independence from his English agents. Therefore he
stopped growing tobacco altogether and increased
Mount Vernon's production of wheat, oats, and corn.

Washington's diaries show that he had a great in-
terest in all things concerning the land. He wrote
about cherry trees, plum trees, and chestnut trees;
the moon, horses, puppies, thunderstorms, and
southerly winds. He recorded his many farm experiments, such as mentioned in one entry from 1760:
"Spent the greatest part of the day making a new
plow of my own Invention."

Washington also tried to grow exotic plants imported from England. He tested different fertilizers
and did experiments with wild grapes. Many years
later he wrote that agriculture "has been the most
favorite amusement of my life."

Washington's daily routine was typical of a gentleman farmer. Every morning he got up at dawn, fixed
his own fire, drank tea, and had cakes of Indian meal.
Then he saddled his horse and rode over his exten-
sive lands. He rode over meadows and hillsides, past
river inlets and wild woods full of deer and fox. He
visited his workers and checked his wheat and corn-
fields, his woodlots and fisheries.

Washington always returned to the main house by
mid-afternoon—in time to prepare to join his family

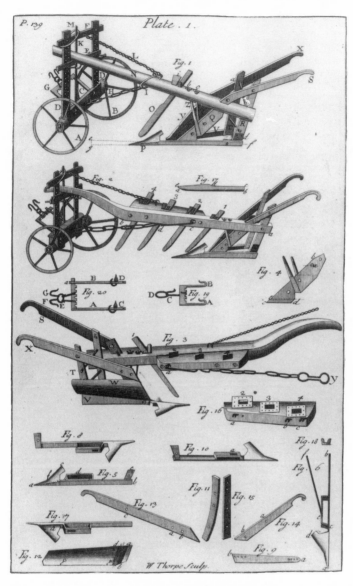

*Jethro Tull's book*, Horse-Hoeing Husbandry, *published in 1733, influenced Washington's early farming experiments. (Beinecke Rare Book and Manuscript Library, Yale University)*

*Washington inspected the Mount Vernon plantation daily on horseback. He once said, "Agriculture is the most healthy, the most useful, and the most noble employment of man." (The Library of Congress)*

and guests for a big dinner. Mount Vernon often had house guests. Records show that in a period of eight years, two thousand people were entertained at the plantation.

Colonial Virginians were famous for their hospitality. As large estates were quite distant from one another, visitors frequently stayed overnight. If Washington did not receive guests for dinner, it usually meant he was dining at someone else's house.

Washington also enjoyed theater and puppet shows. He went fox hunting, game hunting, and fishing. He attended horse races and gambled at cards. The Virginia colony had great elegance and style at that time. One Virginia governor once wrote to England that "the gentlemen and ladies here are perfectly well-bred, and not an ill dancer in my government."

*Martha Washington served refreshments to George and fellow friends after a successful hunt. (The Library of Congress)*

Washington himself is reported to have been a good dancer. He enjoyed balls and often looked in on his stepchildren's dance classes where they learned country dances, as well as the formal minuet.

During the time he was squire of Mount Vernon, Washington was also a burgess—or a representative from his community to the Virginia Assembly.

Though he was a useful member of the Assembly, he was not very outspoken about politics. In fact, his diary during the 1760s gives little hint of the problems growing between England and her American colonies.

At that time there were no British troops on Virginia soil, and colonial life was flourishing. While Mount Vernon's squire was writing cheerfully about plows and fertilizers, however, the American colonies were growing very angry with their mother country.

# A Call to Arms

ϏϾϏ

DURING the French and Indian War the colonists had fought with the British trying to defeat the enemy. But after a treaty was signed in 1763, the colonies began to grow increasingly independent. They no longer felt the need for England's protection. They also began to grow angry at the new taxes imposed by the British.

The English Parliament wanted to collect taxes from the colonies to help pay for the French and Indian War. Until that time the colonists hadn't paid direct taxes to England. Instead they had always voted on their own taxes. But now the English thought the colonies should help pay for the war, for it had been the most expensive in England's history.

Therefore, in 1765 Parliament passed a resolution called the Stamp Act. The Stamp Act forced the colonists to pay taxes on many goods imported from England. The American colonists were outraged.

They said they should not have to pay the taxes because they were not even represented in Parliament. "Taxation without representation is tyranny!" became a familiar slogan.

*This picture of the skull and crossbones reveals the Colonies' feeling about the British Stamp Act of 1765. (The Library of Congress)*

All throughout the colonies, people protested. Secret societies, such as the Sons of Liberty, set out to do away with the Stamp Act. The hated tax actually united the colonies. In October 1765 delegates from nine of the thirteen colonies met to protest together.

A New Method of MACARONY MAKING, as practifed at BOSTON.

*Johnny Malcolm, a spy for the British tax service, was tarred and feathered twice. The first time he was clothed; the second time he was stripped naked, tarred, feathered, and forced to toast all eleven members of the royal family with a cup of tea. (The Library of Congress)*

The colonies were in such an uproar, the Stamp Act was repealed the next year.

However, the English Parliament still wanted to tax the colonies. They passed a new resolution that placed a tax on certain British imports, such as glass, paper, paint, and tea. Once again the colonists were violently opposed to the resolution, and it was repealed.

The British Parliament would not give up. In 1773 it passed the Tea Act. This act ordered that only one English company could sell tea in North America. Colonial merchants were very angry because now their tea could not compete with cheap English tea. On a rainy night in December a band of men disguised as Indians swarmed onto the tea ships in the Boston harbor. The men dumped all the chests filled with tea into the harbor waters.

This act was referred to as the Boston Tea Party and some consider it to be the first act of the American Revolution.

England's prime minister, Lord North, was so furious at the colonists that he closed down the port of Boston. As British troops were installed in Boston, some New England farmers began gathering in the countryside. These farmer soldiers—who called themselves "minutemen"—began piling up weapons and drilling for war.

Though George Washington was very absorbed in his life at Mount Vernon, he did keep a watchful eye on the unrest growing in the American colonies. As a member of the Virginia House of Burgess, he made

*At the Boston Tea Party a band of men disguised as Indians boarded the British tea ships and dumped chests of tea into the Boston harbor. (The Library of Congress)*

a speech in 1765 against the Stamp Act. A few years later he signed a paper, pledging not to purchase most British goods.

But Washington was especially shocked at the harsh British response to the Boston Tea Party. At a Virginia meeting he accused England of tyranny and said that her acts were intolerable.

When a Virginia convention elected seven officials to attend the first Continental Congress in Philadelphia, Washington received the third largest number of votes. In September 1774 he and other colony delegates met to discuss their problems. The delegates finally resolved that if necessary, the colonies would unite and meet the British with force.

Though Washington was fairly quiet at the Congress, he impressed all the delegates. Known as a hero of the French and Indian War, he cut a striking figure. At forty-two his great height and military bearing gave him an air of strength and dignity.

Washington returned to Virginia with a heavy heart. Now it seemed that a call to arms was truly in the air. He dreaded a war with England, for he was very fond of his life at Mount Vernon. He'd worked hard for seventeen years trying to achieve a comfortable and happy life for his family. And now— just when his goals had been achieved—the threat of war had come upon the horizon.

On April 19, 1775, "the shot heard round the world" was fired. In the countryside of Massachusetts, in the villages of Concord and Lexington, British troops met the New England minutemen in battle. More Americans then gathered into an army. Farmers dropped their ploughs, and merchants locked up their shops. Men everywhere picked up their muskets and headed for the Boston area.

A few weeks later Washington returned to Philadelphia for the Second Continental Congress. As he was the only man at the Congress who wore a military uniform, he seems to have been prepared to be

*The minutemen, ordinary citizens who were ready to fight in a moment's notice, fought the British in The Battle of Lexington, 1775. (The Library of Congress)*

elected commander of Virginia's forces. Washington had no idea that the Congress would make him the "General and Commander in Chief of the entire army of the United Colonies."

Washington was both astonished and dismayed when he received a unanimous vote to be commander in chief. In his acceptance speech to the Congress he said, ". . . I this day declare, with the utmost sincerity, I do not think myself equal to the command." And he requested that he not receive a salary for his service, but only receive money for his expenses.

*The Continental Congress, June 15, 1775, elected George Washington commander in chief of the forces raised for the defense of the Colonies. (The Library of Congress)*

In a letter George Washington wrote to Martha from the Congress, he said he would soon be riding north to take command of the whole army. He expressed touching sorrow at being parted from her, and told her his fear of being given such a great responsibility. ". . . I assure you in the most solemn manner that so far from seeking this appointment, I have used every endeavor in my power to avoid it; not only from unwillingness to part with you and the family but from a consciousness of its being a trust too great for my capacity. . . ."

Though he also enclosed his will, Washington wrote that he expected to return home safely by autumn.

Soon after he wrote Martha, General George Washington left Philadelphia on horseback for Boston. Little did he know that it would be six years before he would see his beloved Mount Vernon again.

# Retreat From the Enemy

AFTER THE BATTLES at Concord and Lexington, farmers and merchants from all over the northeast poured into the area surrounding Boston. As this group of about sixteen thousand and six hundred "patriots" formed into the New England army, Washington set out from Philadelphia.

When Washington arrived near Boston in the fall of 1775, he assumed command of the ragtag New England army. The army was untrained and disorderly. There was no staff, no artillery, and no pay chest. As winter approached, Washington's soldiers shivered in their tents and huts. At the end of December many militiamen left when their enlistment period was over. The soldiers who remained had no uniforms and only crude muskets for weapons. They also desperately needed gunpowder. If the redcoats had attacked Washington's men at that time, the redcoats certainly would have won.

The redcoats, however, did not attack. Trapped in Boston beside the cold sea, the British army hoped the colonists would soon come to their senses, give up, and go home. As they waited for more supplies and soldiers to arrive from England, they chopped up buildings to get wood for their fires.

*A Revolutionary War gunpowder horn. (New York Historical Society)*

Washington wanted to force the British out of Boston, but first he needed more weapons. So he sent one of his officers, Colonel Henry Knox, to bring cannons back from two American forts in northern New York. Knox and his men secured about fifty cannons and loaded them onto sledges pulled by eighty pairs of oxen. As they crossed the Berkshire mountains heading back to Washington's camp near Boston, the oxen dragged the sledges over miles of snow and ice.

After the cannons were delivered, Washington ordered two thousand men to haul the big guns to the top of a hill that overlooked the British forces. When the cannons began firing on the city of Boston, the redcoats panicked. Their general ordered them to board warships and sail away to the north.

The patriots were greatly encouraged after the redcoats left Boston. But Washington was certain the British would head for New York next. So in early April he led his men south and began occupying New York City.

In New York, Washington gathered more than twenty-seven thousand men to help set up defenses against the British. He was pleased that his new army now consisted of soldiers from all the colonies and not just New England.

Just as Washington had predicted, the English began to arrive within a couple of months. As they moved into areas surrounding New York, it became apparent that thousands of new recruits had joined the British army. These new recruits were called "Hessians." They were German soldiers hired by the British. Now, with more than thirty thousand men, the British army had many advantages over the American army. It was much wealthier, with more men and supplies. And it had a superior navy, with enough vessels to block the whole American coastline.

What the British army lacked was passion for its cause. Many redcoats did not care whether the British remained in control of the colonies or not. They were only doing their job for the money.

Washington's men, however, were fighting for freedom. A few days after the British arrived in New York, Washington received a copy of the Declaration of Independence. The Declaration, largely the work of a fellow Virginian named Thomas Jefferson, had been adopted in Philadelphia on July 4, 1776.

"When in the course of human events it becomes necessary for one people to dissolve the political bands which have connected them with another, and to as-

*The Declaration of Independence was adopted in Philadelphia on July 4, 1776. A copy was sent and joyfully received by George Washington, who soon read it to his army. (The Library of Congress)*

sume among the Powers of earth the separate and equal station to which the Laws of Nature and Nature's God entitle them . . ."

Until now many soldiers and colonists had hoped that the British and Americans would reach a compromise. But the Declaration made it clear that the Americans wanted to be completely free and independent of England. As Washington began reading the Declaration to his soldiers, he nervously anticipated that some of his men might not agree with it. His worries were put to rest, however, as his men broke into loud cheering when he finished reading the document.

The British continued to arrive in the New York area. And by late August of 1776 the redcoats had attacked the patriots on Long Island, captured more than one thousand men, and killed and wounded many others.

After the Battle of Long Island, Washington decided to retreat to the island of Manhattan. He ordered his men to secretly collect every small boat they could find. And in the middle of a stormy night he led the patriots across the Hudson River. A thick fog helped protect the American army as it crossed the water—almost ten thousand soldiers with their tents, muskets, and even their horses.

In spite of his army's miraculous escape, Washington despaired of remaining in control of New York. When the British began taking over the city, the pa-

*The British redcoats attacked the American patriots in the Battle of Long Island, New York, capturing over one thousand men, and wounding and killing many others. (The Library of Congress)*

triots panicked and fled. Washington furiously galloped after them, but to no avail. He is reported to have thrown his hat down and shouted, "Are these the men with whom I am to defend America?" Not long afterward, Washington wrote to a cousin, "I tell you that I never was in such an unhappy divided state since I was born."

Washington now had only sixteen thousand men, while the British had just received new shiploads of Hessian soldiers—giving them an army of thirty-five thousand men. Things went from bad to worse. Soon after Washington left New York City, he and his men lost the Battle of White Plains. After that battle the

*This 18th-century flintlock, smoothbore musket was a typical weapon used by the British. (New York Historical Society)*

British attacked the American defenses on the Hudson River and took more than twenty-eight hundred patriots as prisoners.

Washington and his men then retreated to New Jersey. Life became a nightmare as the redcoats pursued the commander in chief and his three thousand "broken and dispirited men" across the countryside. Civilians in New Jersey were also terrorized as Hessian soldiers cruelly attacked them and plundered their homes.

Washington finally escaped by leading his sick and freezing men across the Delaware River into Pennsylvania. There the forlorn troops found temporary safety.

At this point many Americans were questioning Washington's ability to lead an army. One of his own generals, Charles Lee, wanted to replace him. Lee had written to someone in Congress, saying that if

MAJ. GEN. LEE.

*Charles Lee*

*General Charles Lee, sent by Congress to assist George Washington, was captured by the British before he reached his post, 1776. (The Library of Congress)*

he had the power, he could do much better than General Washington. Lee also asked the Congress to send more soldiers to him, instead of sending them to Washington.

When Washington was camped in Pennsylvania, General Lee was urged to travel there to assist him. But as Lee advanced across New Jersey to help his commander in chief, he was captured by the British army.

General Lee's capture was a terrible blow to the patriots. Many people believed that Washington could not possibly succeed without the help of Lee. They now thought the war was over—and the British had won.

But just when it seemed that all was lost, General Washington made a brilliant move.

# War Years

❧

O N THE COLD and windy Christmas night of 1776, George Washington led twenty-four hundred soldiers up the edge of the Delaware River. As soon as it got dark, the patriots began climbing into dozens of boats, and in the bitter cold, their boats began crossing the ice-filled Delaware.

Washington's men were heading to Trenton, one of the few British military posts in New Jersey. The commander in chief knew that fifteen hundred Hessian soldiers would be at the fort, celebrating Christmas with drinking and feasting. He knew they would be totally surprised by an attack.

After the patriots disembarked from their boats in the middle of the night, they began the nine-mile trek to Trenton. As they marched over the rough icy ground, some men had no shoes. They only wore old rags tied around their feet. Washington shouted words of encouragement as a bitter winter storm raged

*"Washington Crossing the Delaware" was painted by Emanuel Leutze in Germany, 1851. The boats depicted here are much smaller than the ones Washington used. (The Metropolitan Museum of Art)*

against the battered soldiers, blinding them with rain, snow, and hail. A couple of men even froze to death.

The terrible weather was an advantage, however, for it helped conceal the patriot army. It also convinced the British they were completely safe—no army would march on such a brutal night as this, they thought.

But Washington knew ways of fighting that the British did not know. He'd learned much from the Indians in the French and Indian War. He knew how to surprise the enemy with a hit-and-run attack. At dawn when the patriots struck, the Hessian soldiers were taken completely by surprise. Following European customs of war, they could only fight from formation. And now, blinded by snow, they could not get into formation to fire back at the patriots.

Groggy and dazed from their Christmas celebrating, at least one thousand Hessians were swiftly captured by Washington's army. Only four patriots were lost—and two of them had frozen to death. Washington was very proud of his men. He said their behavior had given him "inexpressible pleasure."

Soon the commander in chief had another success. After Washington's attack on the Hessians, British General Cornwallis and an army of six thousand redcoats marched across New Jersey, determined to punish the patriots. Within a week the British came upon Washington's camp south of Trenton. Since night was falling, General Cornwallis decided to attack the next morning. During the evening, as Cornwallis watched smoke rise from the patriots' fires, he said, "The old fox can't escape this time."

But in the morning the British were stunned to discover that the old fox had indeed escaped. Washington and his men had crept away during the night and marched down the Delaware. In order to fool the British, a few soldiers had been left behind to feed the fires and make noise.

The patriot army then proceeded immediately to nearby Princeton where they surprised another British fort. The redcoats had not expected their arrival, and this time it was Washington's turn to chase a fox. On a tall, white horse as he charged after the fleeing enemy, he shouted, "It's a fine fox chase, my boys!"

The general seemed entirely unaware of danger as he galloped within thirty yards of the enemy action, yelling excitedly to his men. Once again he was miraculously spared from harm.

*The Battle of Trenton, 1776, was a morale-boosting victory for Washington and his troops. (The Library of Congress)*

Washington's victories at Trenton and Princeton lifted the spirits of his army and brought new confidence to the colonists. The victories proved to be a turning point in the Revolutionary War. Americans began to think they might actually succeed in their cause. And the British began to believe that they were not going to win so easily.

In spite of his victories, Washington faced great difficulties that winter. As he and his men camped in Morristown, New Jersey, he desperately tried to recruit more soldiers for his army. If the British had known how small the patriot army really was, they certainly would have been able to defeat them in an attack.

One of the few bright spots at Morristown was the arrival of Martha Washington. Throughout the Revolutionary War, Martha journeyed from Virginia to spend the cold winter months with her husband. Her companionship was always a great relief to him and reminded him of his beloved Mount Vernon.

While the Washingtons and the patriot army wintered in New Jersey, the British chose not to attack. It was not until summer that British troops began moving toward Philadelphia, Pennsylvania. At that time Philadelphia was America's largest city—and also its capital, for it was the home of the Continental Congress.

On July 24, 1777, over two hundred British vessels set sail from New York, heading south for Philadelphia. After the ships docked in the Chesapeake Bay, the redcoats began marching overland toward the patriot capital.

In September, Washington and his troops met the British in a fierce battle at Brandywine Creek near

Chadd's Ford, Pennsylvania. At first it seemed the patriots might win the battle. But then a heavy fog confused the men and caused them to panic. The British won as the patriots were forced from the battlefield.

Members of the Continental Congress fled to York, Pennsylvania, as the British captured Philadelphia. Occupying the area with eight thousand men, the British set about preparing for an attack by the patriots.

But Washington and his army were in no position to attack. Instead, during the winter of 1777 and 1778, they camped on a bleak hill twenty miles outside of Philadelphia. The hilltop was called Valley Forge— a name that would thereafter be associated with hardship and suffering.

That winter at Valley Forge was not only a low point for the patriot army, it was also a terrible time for Washington personally. Again the Congress had begun to lose faith in him and was slow in offering funding. Some even began to think that General Gates, who had won the Battle of Saratoga, would be a better commander in chief. While a group in the Congress was promoting Gates over Washington, and the British were enjoying the comforts of Philadelphia, the American army suffered from a lack of food and shelter and from terrible weather and much illness. In the bitter winter months Washington ordered his men to chop down trees and make cabins

*Washington and his troops spent two icy winters of hardship and suffering on the hilltop called Valley Forge, twenty miles northwest of Philadelphia. (The Library of Congress)*

for shelter. Thomas Paine later wrote that the troops were like "a family of beavers, everyone busy: some carrying logs, others mud, and the rest fastening them together."

Until the cabins were built, the men slept in freezing, smoky tents as icy winds blew outside. Washington tried to get provisions from farms in the countryside, but there was little food to be found. At one point his men ate leather to keep from starving. Some men suffered frostbite so severely that their limbs turned black. Many soldiers had no shoes; wherever they walked, they left bloody footprints in the snow. Disease was rampant, and lice infected the ragged clothing and unwashed hair of the men.

Before the winter was over, more than twenty-five hundred men died at Valley Forge. Washington wrote, "I feel superabundantly for them; and, from my soul, I pity those miseries, which it is neither in my power to relieve or prevent."

Around February things began to brighten a bit. Wagons loaded with meats and vegetables finally arrived from the colonial farmers. Spirits began to improve, so that the men were even able to joke about the miserable conditions and their shabby clothing. Some officers gave a party to which no one was admitted who wore a whole pair of britches.

An amazing Prussian officer from France also helped brighten the dark days at Valley Forge. The officer announced himself as Lieutenant General Friedrich Wilhelm Ludolf Gerhard Augustin Baron von Steuben. Washington wanted the Baron to turn his men into better fighters, to teach them how to march, how to load their guns, and how to use their bayonets.

The patriots grew to love the dramatic little Baron. He had passionate outbursts of anger when they did poorly—and passionate outbursts of joy when they did well. Washington and his officers stood on the sidelines and laughed at the training sessions as if they were viewing first-rate theater.

Benjamin Franklin, the colonists' commissioner to

*Friedrich, Baron von Steuben taught Washington's army how to be better, more efficient fighters. Painting by Charles Willson Peale. (Independence National Historical Park Collection)*

France, and the French war minister had talked Baron von Steuben into going to America to help the patriot army. The French, still angry at the British for defeating them in the French and Indian War, had been sending men and supplies to the patriots to help the cause of freedom. One remarkable French nobleman who volunteered to help the colonists was the Marquis de Lafayette.

Lafayette, though only nineteen years old, loaded a ship at his own expense and sailed it to America. After he landed on the coast of South Carolina, he

*The Marquis de Lafayette brought uniforms and equipment from France to the troops at Valley Forge. Painting by Charles Willson Peale. (Independence National Historical Park Collection)*

hired wagons to carry uniforms and equipment nine-hundred miles to Pennsylvania. When he joined Washington in the summer of 1777, he proved to be a very appealing and magnetic man. His enthusiasm and idealism so touched Washington that a deep bond was formed between them. When Lafayette was injured in his first fight at Brandywine Creek, Washington told the doctors, "Treat him as if he were my son, for I love him as if he were."

In the spring of 1777 as Washington and Lafayette spent their last days at Valley Forge, the French signed a treaty, swearing support for the American cause. Now that France was officially an ally, she promised to send thousands of soldiers and sailors to America. When Washington received the good news, he wrote, "I believe no event was ever received with more heartfelt joy."

# An American Triumph

IN THE SUMMER of 1778 some Philadelphia laundry maids had very interesting news for General Washington. The maids, some of America's most effective spies, reported that the British officers in the city had just ordered their clothes to be returned immediately—washed or unwashed. This could only mean one thing: The British were finally leaving Philadelphia.

The suspicious laundry maids were correct. Very soon afterward the British began leaving the city and heading for New York. As the redcoat army snaked slowly across New Jersey, Washington decided to attack. On a searing hot day in June he ordered General Charles Lee to lead the ambush. General Lee, who had been captured by the British almost two years earlier, had recently been released and was fighting again with Washington.

Some have wondered if General Lee might have

become a turncoat during his capture. Was he secretly trying to help the enemy win the war? On this particular day it seemed that he was, for when General Lee met the British, he ordered his men to retreat.

Washington exploded with fury when he got news of Lee's orders. In the broiling heat, he dashed before the retreating soldiers and ordered them to stop. Lafayette later wrote: "General Washington seemed to arrest fortune with one glance. . . . I thought then as now that I had never beheld so superb a man."

After Washington turned Lee's troops around, the Battle of Monmouth took place. During the fighting,

*After Washington turned General Lee's troops around, the Battle of Monmouth followed. (The Library of Congress)*

Molly Pitcher, the young wife of a cannoneer, brought water to the fighting patriots. When her husband was wounded, she took over firing his cannon. Washington later gave Molly Pitcher a warrant as a noncomissioned officer in the American army.

*Molly Pitcher, a waterbearer for the patriots, took over the firing of her husband's cannon after he was wounded in battle. (The Library of Congress)*

After the Battle of Monmouth, General Lee was court-martialed for giving the disastrous retreat orders to his men. When the Congress expelled him for one year from the service, he grew angry and resigned forever.

While historians cannot prove that Lee was a traitor, they have no doubts about the treason of another general: General Benedict Arnold. The treason of Benedict Arnold was to be one of the greatest surprises and disappointments of Washington's military career. Washington considered Arnold to be an outstanding officer. He even gave Arnold extra attention because he thought he had not been given enough credit for his brave fighting. After the British left Philadelphia, Washington made him military governor of the city. He hoped that this peaceful and pleasant job would help Arnold recover from some of his war wounds.

In Philadelphia, Arnold fell in love with Peggy Shippen, an elegant society belle who was a British sympathizer. Soon after they were married, the Arnolds' grand life-style put them in debt. And at that point they both began to plot with the British.

In exchange for money, Benedict Arnold agreed to help the redcoats capture the American fortress at West Point. West Point on the Hudson River was a very important fort to the Americans. It kept British ocean-going ships from sailing up the Hudson into the American wilderness. General Arnold convinced George Washington to appoint him commander of West Point, and then he set about making a plan to help the British capture the fort.

On September 24, 1780, Washington decided to visit the Arnolds at West Point. When he arrived,

BRIGADIER GEN.ᴸ ARNOLD.

*General Benedict Arnold helped the redcoats capture the American fortress at West Point. (The Library of Congress)*

he was disappointed to find that General Arnold was
not on hand to greet him. Washington did not sus-
pect that earlier that day Arnold had received word
that his plot had been discovered, and he had fled to
avoid capture.

Washington received a letter that afternoon as he
waited at Arnold's home. The letter explained what
had happened and said that the traitor had escaped
to the other side. "Arnold has betrayed us!" Washington reportedly cried out in anguish. "Whom can
we trust now?"

Mrs. Arnold also began shouting—then behaved
as if the news had driven her mad. Of course, she
had been involved in the plot from the beginning.
Her insane ravings convinced Washington she was
innocent, and he sent her back to her family in Philadelphia.

Washington felt great confusion over Benedict Arnold's betrayal. He later said, "My soul is weary of
my life. . . . Changes and war are against me."

During the next year life continued to be grim for
Washington and his army—the American forces were
nearly out of money. On New Year's Day, 1781, thirteen hundred Philadelphia soldiers staged a mutiny.
The soldiers were tired of living in wretched huts
with no pay. They were tired of having no food and
clothing. After the rebels wounded several officers,

General "Mad Anthony" Wayne arrived on the scene and tore open his shirt, then shouted, "If you mean to kill me, shoot me at once!"

The rebels backed off from General Wayne, and eventually he was able to stop the mutiny. But later more troops rebelled in New Jersey. The message was clear to Washington: The American army desperately needed money and supplies. When Washington sent an envoy to France asking for more financial help, he wrote, "We are at the end of our tether."

Meanwhile the patriots in the south were also suffering. An Englishman named Tarleton staged bloody raids in South Carolina, mercilessly slaughtering American soldiers. General Cornwallis, after terrorizing the Carolinas, had moved into Virginia. The traitor Benedict Arnold was now leading redcoat raids on Virginia towns and plantation owners. Washington must have felt great horror when he imagined the hated traitor burning down Mount Vernon. Fortunately his beloved plantation was not attacked.

Finally in July 1781 help came. A great army of French soldiers arrived to help the patriots fight the British. The French in their splendid white uniforms were astonished by the ragged American troops. One Frenchman later wrote: "It is incredible that soldiers composed of men of every age, even of children of fifteen, of whites and blacks, almost naked, unpaid, and rather poorly fed, can march so well and stand fire so steadfastly." The same man wrote of Washington: "He is certainly admirable as the leader of his army, in which everyone regards him as his father and friend."

As a fleet of thirty-six French warships headed for Virginia, Washington and a French general secretly led their armies southward. They marched over four hundred and fifty miles to Virginia. In late September, outside the seacoast town of Yorktown, the French and Americans gathered their forces of nearly seventeen thousand men.

General Cornwallis was camped inside the fortress of the town with an army of only six thousand men. When the Americans and French began shattering the British walls with cannonballs, any hopes of the British winning the battle began to crumble.

Finally, on October 17, the British waved a white handkerchief. Then their drummer boy beat the signal for defeat. Two days later the British surrender was very formal. As British soldiers passed between two rows of American and French troops, the redcoat band played a sad tune called, "The World Turned Upside Down."

General Cornwallis was so bitter about the defeat that he claimed he was too sick to attend the surrender ceremony. He sent another general to hand over his sword. But when the English general tried to give the sword to the French, Washington would not allow it. Finally after Cornwallis's general was forced to surrender to a representative from Washington, the anguished redcoats threw their weapons into a great pile.

*When he was to surrender to Washington, Lord Cornwallis claimed to be ill and his deputy, General O'Hara, surrendered to Washington's deputy, General Lincoln. Painting by John Trumbull. (Yale University Art Gallery)*

During the surrender Washington's ragged, bare-foot soldiers presented a strong contrast to the splendidly dressed French and English soldiers. But the barefoot soldiers had nothing to be ashamed of—for the American triumph at Yorktown marked the end of the Revolutionary War.

After Cornwallis's defeat at Yorktown, peace talks began in Paris. John Jay, Benjamin Franklin, and John Adams were America's Peace Commissioners.

*America's Peace Commissioners*, left to right: *John Jay, John Adams, Benjamin Franklin. Also shown: Henry Laurens and Franklin's grandson, William Temple Franklin, secretary to the American delegation. This painting by Benjamin West was never completed because the British commissioners refused to pose. (The Library of Congress)*

While the talks dragged on for almost two years, the American army stayed together in case the British should surprise them and begin fighting again.

During those two years the American soldiers grew idle and angry. They were mad because they had not been paid, and they were scared of what would happen to them after the war. The soldiers even threatened not to lay down their arms until they were paid.

Washington called his officers together and made a speech, asking them to be patient. As he read the speech, the officers appeared to be unmoved and hostile. But then Washington won them over with a simple gesture. Before he finished his speech, he had difficulty reading, and he stopped to put on a pair of new glasses. As he did this, he said half-sorrowfully, "Gentlemen, you must pardon me. I have grown gray in your service and now find my-self growing blind." This simple statement moved some of the men to tears, and the group's anger was dispelled.

The Peace Treaty was finally signed in September 1783. When the war ended, the thirteen states were still very different from one another. Each was like a separate country with a separate constitution. The colonies had only united for eight years because of the war. Would peace bind them together as well? Many said no—and they thought Washington should seize power and take control of the whole country.

Yet the thought of becoming a king or dictator horrified Washington. Almost every revolution in the world has ended with someone becoming a tyrant or dictator. But Washington wanted the American states to unite and rule themselves. His greatest gift to America was that he did not take advantage of his powerful position. In fact, it has been said that George Washington actually gained more power by giving up power. People all over the world were impressed when they heard that Washington planned to become a farmer again after the war, instead of making himself king. King George III of England said, "If he does that, he will be the greatest man in the world."

In December 1783 General Washington bid goodbye to a group of his officers at a tavern in New York. Major Benjamin Tallmadge later described the meeting. He said that Washington asked all the officers to shake his hand. Then the commander in chief began crying as he grasped each hand and embraced each man in silence. The major wrote: "Such a scene of sorrow and weeping I had never before witnessed . . . that we should see his face no more in this world seemed to me utterly insupportable."

After the tearful embraces, Washington left the room without a word.

*Washington taking leave of his officers, 1783. (The Library of Congress)*

On Christmas Eve, 1783, after eight long years, George Washington returned to Mount Vernon to live. Candles lit all the windows, and Martha and two grandchildren were joyfully waiting to greet the returning soldier.

In the days that followed, happiness overcame Washington. He wrote Lafayette, "I [have] become a private citizen on the banks of the Potomac, and under the shadow of my own vine and my own fig tree . . . I will move gently down the stream of life until I sleep with my fathers."

But Washington was wrong. Fate was not going to allow him to move gently toward his death. Another great role on the world stage was yet to come.

# Mr. President

For the next four years Washington was once again the squire of Mount Vernon. He rose each day and ate his breakfast of "three small Indian hoecakes and as many dishes of tea." Then he mounted his horse and took off across his eight thousand acres of land. Five distinct farms now made up Mount Vernon, and each day Washington visited all of them.

Since his fields needed work after the war, Washington set about again experimenting with different soils and plants. He built a greenhouse, as well as gardens with shady pathways. He tried breeding mules, and he enjoyed his horses and hunting dogs.

One of Washington's great pleasures was spending time with his step-grandchildren, Nelly and Little Washington. They were the children of Martha's son, Jackie, who had died of illness near the end of war. Now they lived most of the time at Mount Vernon.

83

*Washington returned to Mount Vernon after the war. (The Library of Congress)*

As well as taking care of his farms and his family, Washington played host to hundreds of guests in those four years. It was not unusual for twenty people to sit down to dinner with George and Martha. In a single year twenty tons of pork were consumed at Mount Vernon! Visitors from far away frequently stayed overnight at the plantation, including Washington's beloved friend, the Marquis de Lafayette. Since the war Lafayette had named his young son after Washington. The Frenchman's love for America was so strong that years later he carried home boxes of American soil to be buried in.

Artists also visited Mount Vernon in order to paint

pictures of Washington, his family, and home. Since photography had not yet been invented, drawings and paintings were the only way to capture the hero of the Revolutionary War. With his mouth firmly closed, Washington looks quite stern in all of his portraits. Actually he was trying to hide his bad and missing teeth. Years later he was fitted with false teeth made from the ivory teeth of a hippopotamus.

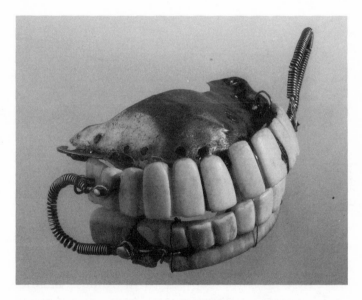

*Washington's false teeth were made of both ivory and human teeth, including one of Washington's own. (The Smithsonian)*

While Washington worked his land and entertained relatives and visitors from all over the world, the United States was struggling to survive. It was a difficult struggle because each state behaved as if it were a different country. Since there was not one central government, there was no way to collect taxes or to reach trade agreements.

During those years Washington tried to keep out of politics, for he wanted America to become strong and democratic without him. He didn't want to ever appear to be seizing power. But as he watched what was going on, he agreed with others that the country needed one central government in addition to the different state governments. He was afraid that the states would soon drift apart and become enemies. He was also afraid the country would never have one united army.

Finally in May 1787 Washington reluctantly agreed to attend the Constitutional Convention in Philadelphia. Even though there were fifty-five other delegates at the convention, Washington was unanimously elected to preside over it.

For four months the delegates debated about the government of the United States. Since they were trying to establish a government that was unlike any other, they had little to guide them. Should there be one main ruler? Should men without property be able to vote? Should the government allow freedom of religion? As the "Founding Fathers" argued and debated with one another, they gradually designed a new government, one such as the world had not seen before.

*Out of fifty-five other delegates Washington was unanimously elected to preside over The Constitutional Convention, 1787. (The Library of Congress)*

Finally the plan for a new constitution was agreed upon. The Constitution, written mostly by a Virginian named James Madison, said that the federal government should have three branches. One branch, the Congress, would make the laws. The Congress would consist of the House of Representatives and the Senate.

Another branch of the government would be the judicial branch. It would be made up of judges who would protect the rights of the people. The third branch, the executive branch, would be the office of president. The president, chosen by electors from each state, was to be elected for a four-year term.

"My movements to the chair of government will be accomplished by feelings not unlike those of a culprit who is going to the place of his execution." These were the feelings Washington expressed to a friend shortly before leaving Mount Vernon to become the first president of the United States. He was worried that the public might not receive him well. He was worried about Martha who was extremely unhappy about leaving Mount Vernon. He was worried about his debts. Washington had so little cash that he was even forced to borrow money to pay for his trip to the nation's temporary capital in New York.

But in April 1789 when Washington left Mount Vernon and headed north to assume office, huge crowds cheered along the way. In Philadelphia nearly twenty thousand people greeted him as he rode his white horse through the city. Everywhere he went, people honored him with speeches, dinners, and parades.

Though Washington heard the wild cheering and shouting, new worries replaced his old ones. He knew that the country desperately needed the right guidance now—or the new government would fail. When he had ridden north years before to be commander in chief, it had been very clear what needed to be done. But now his task was not so clear. How could he keep the states from breaking into different countries? How could he set up a treasury, a postal service, an army, banks, and schools? How could he, a mere soldier and planter, construct and lead a new nation?

*Washington entered New York in 1789 on his way to be sworn in as the first president of the United States of America. (The Library of Congress)*

But the American people were enthusiastic about their new government for only one reason: George Washington. Many people were afraid that one central government would wield too much power. But since Washington was the most loved man in the country, people were willing to try a new government under his leadership.

On April 30, 1789, Washington took the oath of office in New York City. Beside him stood the nation's first vice-president, John Adams. With trembling voice and hands the president gave a short simple speech, which greatly moved everyone.

He said that he wished to be exempted from his salary as president and just be reimbursed for his expenses. Though he intentionally did not use the word "God" in his speech, he expressed gratitude to Providence and an Almighty Being for America's freedom, and he expressed hope that this help and guidance would continue.

How would people address America's new leader? That was one of the first questions to come up after Washington took office. Many thought that "Mr. President" sounded too ordinary. They wanted to call him, "Your Majesty," or "Your Highness," or "Your Excellency." All those names disturbed Washington. He wanted to be known only as "Mr. President."

Washington was also horrified the first time his aide introduced him to a roomful of visitors. The aide threw open the door and shouted, "The President of the United States!" Washington thought it sounded as if a king were making an entrance. He

*Washington took the presidential oath of office in New York City on April 30, 1789. John Adams, the first vice-president of the United States, stood behind Washington. (The Library of Congress)*

angrily told his aide never to announce him that way again.

After putting things in order at Mount Vernon, Martha Washington joined George in New York, and they began having weekly receptions, dinners, and

*Martha Washington held weekly presidential receptions. (The Library of Congress)*

tea parties. Every Tuesday, President Washington had a reception for men only. Any man who was properly dressed could attend. Washington usually stood uncomfortably at these receptions, holding his dress hat and wearing his sword under his black dress coat.

It's been said President Washington much preferred Martha's relaxed tea parties that were held every Friday. There he carried neither a sword nor a hat. Abigail Adams, the wife of Vice-President Adams, reported after a tea party that Washington was "polite with dignity, affable without familiarity, distant without haughtiness, grave without austerity, modest, wise, and good."

Abigail Adams also admired the First Lady. She described Martha as "plain in her dress, but the plainness is the best of every article. . . . Her hair is white, her teeth beautiful. . . . Mrs. Washington is one of those unassuming characters which create love and esteem."

The Washingtons did not stay in New York for very long. In the summer of 1790 plans were made to build a Federal City near Mount Vernon. Since the Federal City, now known as Washington, D.C., would take ten years to be built, the capital was temporarily moved to Philadelphia.

During his first years in office Washington took coach trips to New England and the southern states. In the north he saw ships, factories, and farms with fields of wheat and red corn. In the south he saw pine barrens and fields of tobacco and rice. As he moved unannounced through small, dusty southern towns, innkeepers and tavern owners were astonished when his carriage would pull up to their door.

One of Washington's most important jobs as president was to choose the right people to help him. Besides the three hundred and fifty workers already employed as government clerks and secretaries, he needed a group of close advisors.

When he first entered office, Washington chose Alexander Hamilton to be his secretary of the treasury. He made General Henry Knox the first secretary of war. And he appointed Edmund Randolph as the first attorney general. To handle the country's foreign affairs, Washington made Thomas Jefferson the secretary of state. Jefferson, the author of the Declaration of Independence, was also a plantation owner in Virginia who had many of the same farming interests as Washington.

Hamilton, Knox, Randolph, and Jefferson—these men made up the first "cabinet" of the United States. Washington had hoped that his cabinet members would get along with one another, but he was sadly disappointed. In the first year of his presidency Jefferson and Hamilton began a conflict that grew more and more heated as time went by. Not only did the two men compete for Washington's affections, but they also represented different interests of the country. Hamilton stood for the northern businessmen who wanted a strong central government, and Jefferson stood more for the farmers and ordinary citizens who feared that a powerful central government

*Washington's Cabinet*, from left to right, *General Henry Knox (secretary of war)*, *Thomas Jefferson (secretary of state)*, *Edmund Randolph (attorney general)*, *Alexander Hamilton (secretary of the treasury)*, and *President Washington. (The Library of Congress)*

would lead to a monarchy. Washington tried to make peace between the two, but their differences could not be easily resolved.

Washington was sixty years old when it was time for his first term as president to end. Longing to return to Mount Vernon, he told Jefferson that "he felt himself growing old . . . and tranquility and retirement [had become] an irresistible passion."

But Jefferson, along with others, urged Washington to stay on for a second term. Jefferson told him that the "North and South will hang together if they have you to hang on to." In order to help smooth over the many problems of the new government, Washington did not step down from office, and he was unanimously reelected on February 13, 1793.

# A Hero's Farewell

كمكم

SOON AFTER Washington was reelected, the French king and queen were beheaded by the people of France. France's poor people had suffered terrible injustices, until they finally rose up in revolt. After the French monarchs were executed, a reign of terror began in that country. Then France declared war on England, Spain, and Holland.

Americans supported the French Revolution—it reminded them of their own fight for freedom and equality. They were also grateful to France for helping them win the Revolutionary War. Many Americans, including Thomas Jefferson, wanted the United States to get involved and help the French revolutionaries.

But Washington insisted the United States should remain neutral. He believed a war with France against England would destroy the tender growth of a new nation. He said America should concern itself with its own problems.

Many people criticized Washington's position and accused him of favoring royalty. Newspapers attacked him, and other politicians turned against him. Much later, however, the country realized he had made a wise decision not to get involved. The new American government did indeed have enough problems of its own to contend with.

One major problem Washington faced was the Whiskey Rebellion. A group of independent frontiersmen in western Pennsylvania had grown angry about a tax placed on homemade whiskey. The farmers did not want to give the government their money; they also resented tax collectors coming onto their land. They grew so angry, they beat and tortured the collectors. The Allegheny farmers roamed the countryside in drunken bands, burning the homes of innocent people who paid the whiskey tax. The violence grew as more mountain men became involved. The rebellious men even threatened to separate from the United States and start their own country.

Though the farmers were fierce and determined, Washington refused to give into their demands. When he sent nearly thirteen thousand militiamen to stop the revolt, the farmers gave up "without a drop of blood."

*Angry farmers rampaged against whiskey tax collectors during the Whiskey Rebellion. (Historical Pictures Collection)*

The following year Washington faced more conflict when he supported the Jay Treaty. The Jay Treaty was an agreement made by Chief Justice John Jay with the English. Many people thought that it gave too many rights to the British. Washington thought so too, but to avoid war with England, he supported the treaty. Again the newspapers criticized him, saying he didn't know how to govern.

Washington had never suffered in the battles of war as he now suffered in the battles of politics.

Though he was a man of great physical and emotional strength, he was very sensitive to criticism. He began to doubt himself; he even worried that he might be losing his mental abilities.

When his second term ended, Washington chose not to run again, and Vice-President John Adams was elected the second president of the United States.

*John Adams became the second president of the United States in 1797. (The Library of Congress)*

Besides feeling tired and discouraged, Washington believed an American president should not serve for more than eight years. Oddly, leaving office was one of his greatest contributions to America's future. Washington proved that the country did not need a king or a dictator in order to succeed, and that electing presidents for a given period of time was a workable plan.

Washington's Farewell Address also greatly affected America's future. In a simple yet touching speech he repeated the idea that the states should remain united and neutral. He said that the country needed to take care of itself and not get involved in foreign wars. Americans should be *Americans*, he said, and not English or French.

Of course, Americans could not hear Washington's message on television or radio in those days. But newspapers quoted his entire speech. And as time went on, his words had an almost magical effect. They helped to strongly shape United States foreign policy for the next one hundred and fifty years.

Though Washington left in the midst of conflict and criticism, most people mourned his departure from office. In spite of all the controversy, they still supported the national hero and wished that he would continue to lead them.

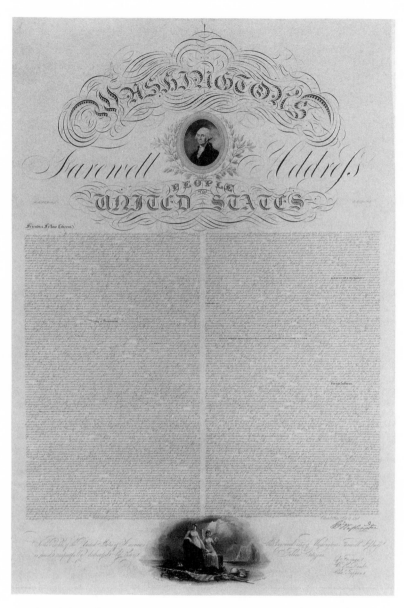

*An early 19th-century engraving of Washington's Farewell Address.*
*(The Granger Collection)*

In March 1797 when Washington returned to Mount Vernon, he found the plantation in great need of repair. He set to work immediately, planning its reconstruction. He soon wrote a friend that there was hardly a room without the sound of hammers or the smell of paint.

As usual, Washington found himself struggling with money problems. Nearly all of his life he had worried about his finances and had been afraid of getting into huge debt. At that time a president received no retirement salary or pension money. Washington hated the idea of selling his slaves because he didn't want to break up their families. So, in order to take care of his home and all his slaves, he sold some of his land.

Though he was sixty-four years old when he returned to Mount Vernon, Washington resumed his long horseback rides over his plantation grounds. He ended his days with dinner, a walk, and tea. At "candlelight" he and Martha took leave of their ever-present guests and retired.

In 1798 Washington was suddenly called back to duty. President Adams, facing problems with the French government, asked Washington to become commander in chief again.

Washington did not have to go on active duty, but he did help plan the new army. One of his favorite activities was helping to design the army's uniforms.

*Washington discussing haying with a Mount Vernon worker.*
*(The Library of Congress)*

Ever since he'd been a boy, he'd been interested in military regalia. Now for himself he designed a blue coat with yellow buttons and silver stars. He eagerly looked forward to the arrival of the uniform so he could wear it to the wedding of his favorite step-granddaughter, Nelly. But when Washington's uniform arrived, it was too small and had to be sent back to the tailor to be fixed. Sadly, he was never to have the pleasure of wearing it.

On a cold December day in 1799, as Washington rode across his grounds on horseback, it began to snow. Then it began to hail, and finally a cold rain fell. When he returned home, his secretary, Tobias Lear, observed that Washington's "neck appeared wet and the snow was hanging on his hair."

The next day there was more snow and wind. Washington stayed inside because his throat was sore. Though hoarse, he sat up in the evening, reading the papers and talking cheerfully with Martha and Tobias Lear.

Late in the night Washington woke Martha and said he felt very unwell. His throat was in terrible pain. Doctors were immediately called for. In the meanwhile Washington almost suffocated when he tried to swallow a mixture of molasses, vinegar, and butter given him to ease the pain in his throat.

Martha sat near the foot of his bed as Washington told his doctors to cut his arm and "bleed" him. Bleeding was a common medical practice in those days. People thought they could get well by ridding their bodies of impure blood. Many historians think now that Washington had a throat infection that to-day would be cured with penicillin. But in those days there were no such antibiotics to fight infections. And taking blood from Washington only made him weaker.

Tobias Lear later wrote that Washington finally said to his doctors, "I feel myself going. I thank you for your attention. You had better not take any more trouble about me but let me go off quietly. I cannot last long."

He did not complain during his final hours, but

near the end Washington grew afraid that he might
be buried alive. He made Tobias Lear promise that
he would not be put in his burial vault for less than
two days after he died. Then around midnight on

*An unfinished sketch by an unknown artist shows Washington on
his deathbed, attended by two doctors and Martha. (The New
York Historical Society)*

December 14, 1799, George Washington, without a
struggle, slipped quietly into death.

The whole country grieved over the loss of George
Washington. Black headlines appeared in all the papers, and Congress declared an official day of
mourning. On that day Henry Lee, a respected sol-

dier in the American Revolution and member of Congress, delivered a eulogy. Of his dear friend George Washington, Lee said, "First in war, first in peace, and first in the hearts of his countrymen, he was second to none."

*"The American Star"* painted by Frederick Kemmelmeyer of Baltimore, Maryland, showed American reverence for the hero and father of the country. (*The Metropolitan Museum of Art*)

# TIMELINE OF
# GEORGE WASHINGTON'S LIFE

1732   In February, born in Virginia colony to Augustine and Mary Washington

1738   In December, moved to Ferry Farm on the Rappahannock

1743   In April, father died

1748   In March, left for thirty-three day surveying trip through Shenandoah Valley

1751   In September, went with brother Lawrence to West Indies; caught smallpox

1752   In July, Lawrence died of tuberculosis

1753   In October, left for mission to Fort Le Boeuf in Ohio Valley to warn French away

1755   In July, hero of General Braddock's defeat in Ohio Valley
       In August, appointed commander of all the Virginia troops

1759  In January, married Mrs. Martha Dandridge
      Custis; became stepfather to Patsy and Jackie
      Custis

1765  In October, delivered a speech against the Stamp
      Act to the Virginia House of Burgess

1774  In September, attended First Continental
      Congress in Philadelphia, Pennsylvania

1775  In May, attended Second Continental Congress
      in Philadelphia
      In June, elected commander in chief of "all the
      continental forces" to fight the Revolutionary
      War against the British
      In July, assumed command of sixteen thousand
      and six hundred men at Cambridge, Massa-
      chusetts

1776  In April, set up defenses in New York City
      In July, read the Declaration of Independence to
      his troops
      In December, crossed the Delaware River in
      Trenton to attack Hessian soldiers

1777  In January, set up winter quarters in Morris-
      town, New Jersey
      In December, moved men to Valley Forge, near
      British-occupied Philadelphia

1780  In September, discovered treason of General
      Benedict Arnold

1781   In August, started south toward Virginia,
          followed by French army
       In October, defeated General Cornwallis's troops
          at Yorktown

1783   In May, announced official end of the war to his
          men
       In December, resigned as commander in chief;
          returned to Mount Vernon

1787   In May, elected president of the Constitutional
          Convention in Philadelphia

1789   In February, electors unanimously voted Wash-
          ington first president of the United States
       In April, left Mount Vernon for New York to
          begin serving first term

1793   In March, inaugurated for a second term as
          president
       In March, word arrived from France of execution
          of Louis XVI in January; France at war

1794   In September, orders troops to suppress the
          Whiskey Rebellion

1795   In August, signed the Jay Treaty

1797   In March, attended inauguration of John Adams,
          then returned to Mount Vernon

1799   In December, died at Mount Vernon, probably
          of a throat infection

# BIBLIOGRAPHY

ALDEN, JOHN. *George Washington, A Biography.* Louisiana State University Press, 1984.

BLIVEN, BRUCE, JR. *The American Revolution.* New York: Random House, 1986.

CUNLIFFE, MARCUS. *George Washington, Man and Monument.* New York: Little, Brown and Co., 1958.

DONOVAN, FRANK. *The George Washington Papers.* New York: Dodd, Mead & Co., 1964.

FLEXNER, JAMES THOMAS. *George Washington in the American Revolution.* Boston: Little, Brown and Co., 1967.

———. *Washington, the Indispensable Man.* Boston: Little, Brown and Co., 1974.

FOSTER, GENEVIEVE. *George Washington's World.* New York: Scribners, 1946.

FREEMAN, DOUGLAS SOUTHHALL. *George Washington,* Volume One. New York: Scribners, 1948.

JONES, ROBERT F. *George Washington.* Twayne Publishers, 1979.

KENT, ZACHARY. *George Washington.* Children's Press, 1986.

OSBORNE, LUCRETIA PERRY. *Washington Speaks for Himself.* New York: Scribners, 1972.

*The Papers of George Washington.* Colonial Series, 1983.

REEDER, COLONEL RED. *The French and Indian Revolution.* Thomas Nelson, Inc., 1972.

―――. *The Story of the Revolutionary War.* Duell, Sloan and Pearce, 1959.

THANE, ELSWYTH. *Potomac Squire.* Duell, Sloan and Pearce, 1963.

WILLS, GARY. *Cincinnatus.* New York: Doubleday, 1984.

# INDEX

# ABOUT THE AUTHOR

Mary Pope Osborne has published four previous novels for young adults with Dial: *Run, Run, As Fast As You Can; Best Wishes, Joe Brady; Love Always, Blue;* and *Last One Home.* Of *Last One Home, School Library Journal* wrote, "Finely crafted characterization enhances this affecting story." Ms. Osborne demonstrated her novelist's skill in characterization with her most recent biography, *The Many Lives of Benjamin Franklin,* also published by Dial. Praised by *Publishers Weekly* as "thoroughly researched and comprehensive," *The New York Times Book Review* wrote that Benjamin Franklin himself "might well have been pleased at this handsome account of his life."

Ms. Osborne grew up on Army posts throughout the country, mostly in the South. She now divides her time between New York City and Bucks County, Pennsylvania, with her husband Will and her dog Bailey.